AN ENCHANTMENT OF

ELEPHANTS

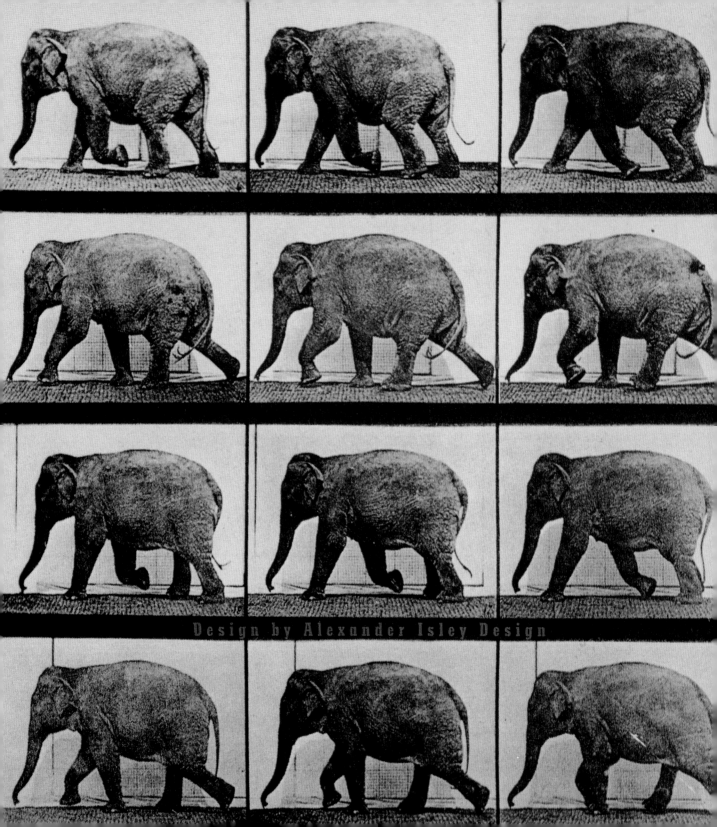

Design by Alexander Isley Design

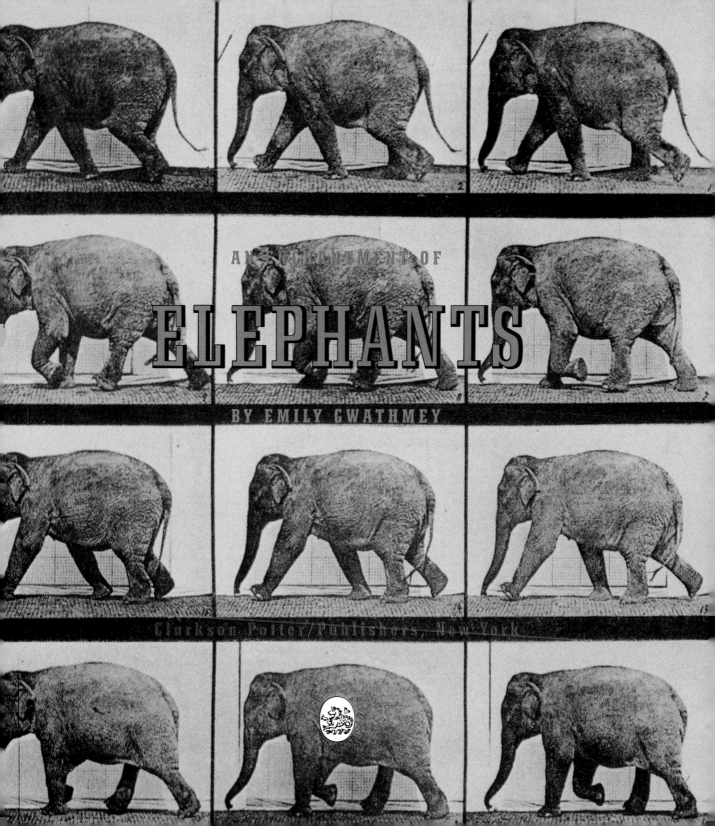

AN ENCHANTMENT OF

ELEPHANTS

BY EMILY GWATHMEY

Clarkson Potter/Publishers, New York

FOR
MARSHALL BEIL

UNSTINTINGLY SUPPORTIVE, UNFORGETTABLY KIND

Published by Clarkson N. Potter, Inc., 201 East 50th Street, New York, New York 10022.
Member of the Crown Publishing Group.
Random House, Inc. New York, Toronto, London, Sydney, Auckland

CLARKSON N. POTTER, POTTER, and colophon are trademarks of Clarkson N. Potter, Inc.

Manufactured in Japan

Library of Congress Cataloging-in-Publication Data

Gwathmey, Emily.
An enchantment of elephants by Emily Gwathmey.
Includes bibliographical references.
1. Elephants–Folklore. 2. Elephants–History. I. Title.
GR730.E44G83 1993   93-18046
398'. 369961–dc20

ISBN 0-517-59184-7

10 9 8 7 6 5 4 3 2 1

Contents

Elephants are contagious.
—Surrealist proverb

Once elephants traveled the earth in vast colonies, "an ancient life force," wrote Peter Matthiessen, "delicate and mighty, awesome and enchanted, commanding the silence ordinarily reserved for mountain peaks, great fires, and the sea." Respected for their trainability and physical versatility, elephants have long been revered as "pillars of the universe," "beasts of the moon," and "nature's great masterpiece." But these socially sophisticated gentle giants have the sad misfortune of possessing a treasure—their "white gold" ivory tusks—coveted by greedy humans since the beginning of history. The tragic result is that the world's most massive and intriguing terrestrial mammal is now in imminent danger of extinction.

Elephants and people have a long and intertwined history. Actually, despite the obvious differences in appearance, elephants and people are very much alike. Both are smart, although the elephant's highly convoluted brain—thought to be a sign of intelligence—is about twice the size of a human's. (Perhaps this accounts for its extraordinary memory.) Both live in complicated social structures. (The elephant's is a hierarchical herd composed of matriarchal clans ruled by an elder female; after adolescence, adult males roam the outskirts of the group, mingling with the family clans only when they feel the urge to mate.) Both enjoy long life spans. Both are susceptible to diabetes, colds, pneumonia, and the mumps.

Both elephants and people are highly emotional. Certainly both display affection, but they also show compassion, tenderness, humor, and grief. Elephants greet each other warmly after a short separation (entwined trunks is analogous to a kiss) and mourn the loss of clan members. Both love touching, playing, bathing (elephants favor mud baths whenever possible, to keep cool and bug free), and communicating, something elephants do by grunting, rumbling, bellowing, trumpeting, or emitting mysterious, deep, low-pitched, infrasound noises that only other elephants can hear. Both love to eat, although all elephants are strict vegetarians. "Elephant grass," a tall herbaceous plant, is

INTRODUCTION

their favorite food, part of major nourishment needs that can mount up to 350 pounds a day, plus 30 to 50 gallons of water.

And then there is the elephant's trunk, a distinctive anatomical feature that has no human, or animal, counterpart. In 1886 a British writer named Nott penned an eloquent description: "This trunk is composed of a mass of interlacing muscles, marvellously arranged, numbering, Cuvier estimates, nearly forty thousand. Some running longitudinally and others radiating from the center to the circumference, all so beautifully combined and adjusted to give it flexibility and strength, enabling it to be expanded or contracted, or wielded with that diversity of motion, and used in these manifold ways that must excite amazement when first seen, and from time immemorial have made the elephant's trunk an object of wonder and admiration." One tale from Rudyard Kipling's <u>Just So Stories</u>

describes the mythical "high and far-off times" when the Elephant Child met a crocodile at the bank of the great, gray-green, greasy Limpopo River. During a tug-of-war between the two animals, the Elephant Child's small button nose was stretched into its present-day length. But however the trunk is described, and however it came about, its degree of dexterity enables an elephant to pick a delicate bouquet of flowers or pick up a single hairpin.

Elephant legs are thick and sturdy as tree trunks, yet graceful. The Greek rhetorician Aelian describes a show given by Germanicus around A.D. 12 in which elephants wearing flowing garments danced and whirled about in perfect rhythm while strewing flowers delicately on the floor. Because of their bone construction, elephants actually walk on the tips of their toes and are both agile and quiet. They can amble at 30 MPH—"pacing along as if they had an appointment at the end of the world," Isak Dinesen wrote—and manipulate their awkward bodies into headstands a yogi master would envy. Elephants cannot jump (perhaps that is just as well), but they <u>can</u> negotiate steep slopes and record astonishing cross-country mileage.

Of the 325 species of elephants that once wandered the continents, only two remain: the African <u>Loxodonta</u>, both forest and bush types, and the Asian or Indian <u>Elephas maximus</u>. The social habits of the two species are similar, although their physiognomy differs markedly. Africans are enormous. An average male stands 10½ feet tall at the shoulder and weighs about 12,000 pounds, with oversize ears roughly resembling

To dream of an elephant
means you will be rich.
—The Oracle

The world's largest elephant skeleton.

The Moab mastodon, carved on a canyon wall in Utah.

Life-size replica of an American mastodon.

freehand maps of Africa. The smaller Asiatic elephants (whose females do not develop tusks) usually stand no more than 9 feet high and weigh a mere 10,000 pounds. Their ears are modest-size and look a lot like a map of India. Differently shaped backs and foreheads, number of toenails, and construction of trunk tip—Asian trunks have one "finger" at the end, African two—further distinguish the two species.

Elephants are vanishing rapidly. Their natural habitats have been fragmented by the mindless destruction of forests and grazing lands, recently accelerated by the drought in Africa. The elephants that remain have been mercilessly hunted by ivory poachers, motivated by the large profit to be made in the trade of "white gold."

The ivory trade is as old as civilization. Ivory's glistening sheen and malleable properties make it a superior material for creating articles of adornment. "Thrones of ivory stretch across the ages," E. D. Moore recorded in his 1931 book, "for there is the ivory throne of Solomon, the ivory throne sent by Hezekiah, king of Judah, as tribute to Sennacherib, the throne of ivory sent to the Etruscan king Porsenna, and the ivory throne sent from Travancore by its Indian prince to his empress, Victoria of Britain. Perhaps we should include the ivory chair, inlaid with gold, of Suleiman the Magnificent, in which he sat while, on the feast of Bairam, all the harem women came to kiss the unspeakable Turkish foot." Ivory (often worked into intricate inlays and elaborate carvings) has been used for millennia in jewelry and other luxury items, as well

Seeing no other elephants around, I rose and perceived that I was on a little hill of some breadth, entirely covered with bones and teeth of elephants. I admired the instinct of these animals and did not doubt that this was their cemetery or place of burial, and that they had brought me hither to show it to me, that I might desist from destroying them, as I did it merely for the sake of possessing their teeth.

—*The Seventh and Last Voyage of Sinbad the Sailor*

as more pedestrian caskets, book covers, religious relics, walking sticks, boxes, combs, netsukes, billiard balls, and piano keys.

Originally elephants were hunted primarily for their meat; the tusk was valued simply as a by-product. Organized ivory trading, however, dates back to the Phoenicians and developed into a large-scale operation during the European colonization of Africa. Beginning in the sixteenth century, the ivory trade grew in conjunction with the slave trade. Indeed, ivory was initially more valuable than the slaves who carried it. (The "Ivory Coast" in West Africa was named for the first major source of supply.) Over the centuries the trade has grown dramatically and has left the elephant population decimated. African elephants numbered 10,000,000 in 1940. Now there are 625,000. In Asia, only 40,000 elephants remain. Great elephant families

that once roamed the planet in harmony with heaven and earth have been brought to the edge of extinction.

In many ways, the fate of the elephant parallels the fate of Native American Indians. Both societies lived close to nature until, in the name of progress and greed, they became victims of unconscionable brutality, driven from their lands, forced to live on reservations, doomed to suffer unspeakable indignities. In 1884, Chief Seattle of the Nez Percé spoke prophetic words: "What happens to beasts will happen to man. All things are connected. If the great beasts are gone, man would surely die of a great loneliness of spirit."

This book is a celebration of the greatest of beasts. My personal enchantment began one night in a dream in which I was journeying through an exotic landscape on the back of an elephant. Then, while awake, I began noticing that their likenesses, whether flat or three-dimensional, were everywhere—in museums and store displays, on T-shirts and shopping bags, in art galleries

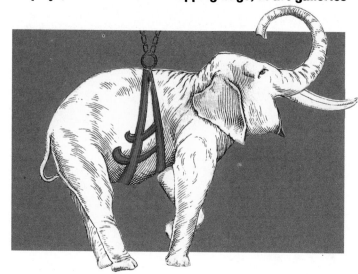

and card shops, in flea markets and magazine ads. My base of operation is the cityscape of Manhattan, and when one spring day I serendipitously happened upon the remarkable annual parade of circus elephants through Central Park, I surrendered. The elephants were calling me, and I felt compelled to answer.

As a deltiologist and ephemerist (collector of postcards and printed matter), I began to search for elephant imagery. The depth and breadth of what I found was mind-bending and forms the basis of <u>An Enchantment of Elephants</u>. I discovered extraordinary pictures of elephants in all their endearingly wrinkled splendor—in the jungle, at the zoo, giving rides to children and kings, performing in the circus, the theater, and the water, at work, at play, and at war. I unearthed elephants comical, political, commercial, architectural, and mythological. In this book I have tried to include as many different facets of elephantine impact on human society as possible.

In many cultures, elephants are symbols of good luck. Figures of elephants are set facing doorways to ward off evil, and replicas are employed as ornaments and lucky charms. A trunk upward is said to hold in good luck, and the trunk hanging down pours out blessings wherever it points. Perhaps this modest contribution to history's celebration of the world's most massive and intriguing mammal—now tragically endangered—will help sustain elephant luck, so that elephants may continue to exist as universally revered animals in the wild, as well as in mythology, religion, art, literature, and popular culture.

THE ELEPHANT IS SLOW TO MATE

The elephant, the huge old beast,
    is slow to mate;
he finds a female, they show no haste
    they wait

for the sympathy in their vast shy hearts
    slowly, slowly to rouse
as they loiter along the river-beds
    and drink and browse

and dash in panic through the brake
    of forest with the herd,
and sleep in massive silence, and wake
    together, without a word.

So slowly the great hot elephant hearts
    grow full of desire,
and the great beasts mate in secret at last,
    hiding their fire.

Oldest they are and the wisest of beasts
    so they know at last
how to wait for the loneliest of feasts
    for the full repast.

They do not snatch, they do not tear;
    their massive blood
moves as the moon-tides, near, more near,
    till they touch in flood.

—D. H. Lawrence

The ELEPHANT *Sublime*

Mythic Beasts

Elephants appear prominently within the complex pantheon of Indian mythology, and several Hindu legends suggest the origin of elephants. In one, the divine milk-white elephant Airavata, royal steed of the god Indra, was created by Brahma and related through his mother to the life fluid of the cosmos.

Another myth holds that Airavata and the other original elephants appeared out of the Churning of the Milky Ocean endowed with wings and the power to roam freely through the sky. An angry saint called upon the gods to deprive elephants of their wings after the animals fell from a tree and killed several of his students. Yet earthbound elephants were popular and honored attractions at Hindu courts. It was believed they still had the power to call upon their former celestial companions and attract clouds to insure life-giving rain and prosperity.

Ganesha, son of the god Shiva, is a short, potbellied, elephant-headed male, the benevolent lord of wisdom and good fortune and remover of obstacles. The most popular of Hindu gods, he is always depicted missing one tusk, which he may have used to transcribe the *Mahabharata*, or which he may have thrown at the moon when it laughed at his uncontrollable sweet tooth.

Ganesha often rides on or is accompanied by a rat, portraying his spiritual strength over the demonic forces symbolized by the rodent. His four hands generally hold a conch shell, a discus, a hatchet (symbol for the cutting away of illusion), and a lotus. Around his stomach he wears a serpent, as a sacred thread.

Gajendra, lord of the elephants, was believed to have been a king in his former life. When Gajendra entered a watering hole one day to quench his thirst, a serpent coiled itself around his legs and trapped the animal lord. Raising a lotus flower in his trunk, Gajendra sang praise to Vishnu, who killed the serpent and rescued him.

"Praise to thee,
O Ganesha.
Thou art manifestly
the truth…
the Supreme Brahma,
the eternal spirit."

All Hindu undertakings, great and small, from school exam to journey's start to religious rite, begin with this invocation.

Gajendra sings to Vishnu, above. The seven trunks of Airavata are associated with the number seven in multiple aspects: the types of desire, the basic color spectrum, the major planets. The seven male

and eight female elephants born at the same time as Airavata became the ancestors of all elephants and are considered to be the pillars of the universe. The blue winged elephant is the logo designed by Milton Glaser for The Overlook Press.

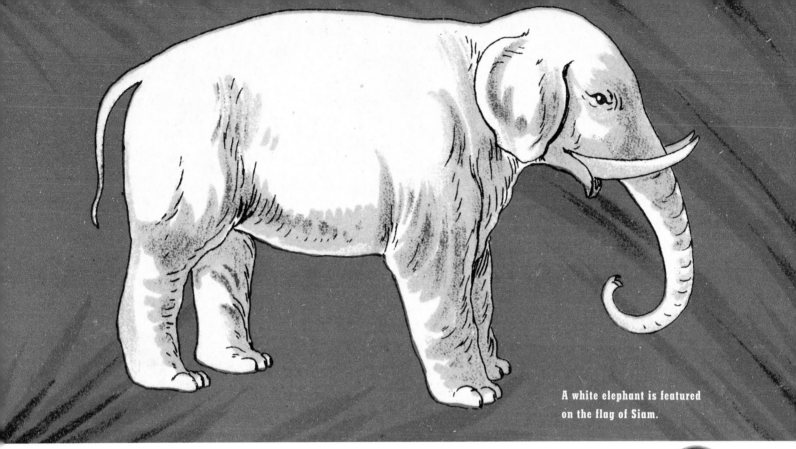

A white elephant is featured
on the flag of Siam.

The Sacred White

Buddhists revere the rare white elephant as the holiest of beasts, the very embodiment of the soul of Buddha, as myth holds that the Buddha's conception occurred when his mother dreamed of being impregnated by a six-tusked white elephant.

The depiction of a pair of pure white elephants bathing and purifying the goddess Lotus, mother of the earth, is a recurring feature of early Buddhist art. The elephants represent the clouds and rain that fall at her behest. The form under which Buddha will descend to the earth for the last time "will be that of a beautiful young white elephant, open-jawed, with a head the color of cochineal, with tusks shining like silver sparkling with gems, covered with a splendid netting of gold, perfect in its organs and limbs, and majestic in appearance."

In Thailand, white elephants are treated as living gods. In 1861 the king of Siam, one of whose titles was "Lord of the White Elephant"—the word *Siam* means "Land of the Sacred White Elephant"—founded the royal order of "the White Elephant." Each year the anniversary of this event is reason for great celebration. White elephants are bathed in pure water, doused with perfume, and painted head to toe in rainbow color. With tusks adorned with gold and bodies bedecked with jeweled robes, necklaces, and pendants, the elephants are paraded through the streets, where the populace falls to its knees in worship.

Most Royal Elephant! We beg that you will not think too much of your mother and father . . . (or) regret leaving your native forests, because there are evil spirits there . . . and wild beasts that howl. And that is not all, in the forest you have no servants, and it is very unpleasant to sleep with dust and filth adhering to your body.

—ANNA LEONOWENS

the emperor

sleeps in a palace of porphyry

which was a million years building

he takes the air in a howdah

of jasper beneath saffron

umbrellas

upon an elephant

twelve feet high

behind whose ear

sits always a crowned

king twirling an

ankus of

ebony

the fountains of the emperor's

palace run sunlight and

moonlight and the emperor's

elephant is a thousand years old

—E. E. CUMMINGS

In ancient times, owning an elephant was the prerogative of kings—certainly the expense of housing and feeding one was something only royalty could afford. In many Asian countries today, royalty still employs elephants as carriers of supplies and people. On state occasions elaborate canopied howdahs are strapped to their backs.

In Sri Lanka, during the week before the full moon in August, the finest elephant of all— always named Raja (for King) —is honored with the job of bearing a casket containing the sacred Tooth Relic of the Lord Buddha, in the world-famous 500-year-old Kandy Perahera ceremonial procession through the streets of the capital city.

HERR SCHOLZ AND HIS WONDER ELEPHANT "MARY ELLEN."

ON THE JOB AT WORK AND AT WAR

Since man began domesticating animals, elephants have been tireless and compliant servants to the whims of humans. The animals' prodigious strength combined with an astonishingly high degree of trainability have made them unequaled as tanks, transporters, haulers, hunters, and performers.

In Asia elephants were once widely used as mounts for hunters of tigers and lions. Today Asian elephants are employed primarily as beasts of burden in the timber industry. Trained for haul-

THE ELEPHANT MUNDANE

INDIA—FORT ON THE INDUS.

ing and piling logs, elephants are uncannily adept workers with extraordinary pushing and pulling strength. Elephants have also been pressed into service as mail carriers during and after rainy seasons and as draft animals whose singular strength substitutes for that of a team of six horses. Pairs of elephants supporting a platform stage upon their backs on which dancers, jugglers, and clowns cavort provided the foundation for a popular form of street theater in Indochina and Ceylon.

Warrior elephants were once of major importance in both the East and the West. King Porus of India amassed elephants in a battle against Alexander the Great; Pyrrhus, king of Epirus, and the Persian general Darius also deployed the living

L'ÉLÉPHANT: Les éléphants de Pyrrhus.

VÉRITABLE EXTRAIT DE VIANDE LIEBIG.

L'ÉLÉPHANT: L'éléphant au travail.

VÉRITABLE EXTRAIT DE VIANDE LIEBIG.

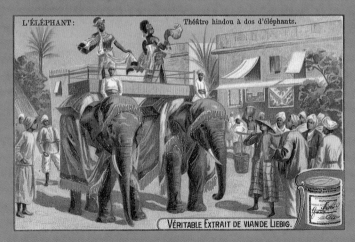

L'ÉLÉPHANT: Théâtre hindou à dos d'éléphants.

VÉRITABLE EXTRAIT DE VIANDE LIEBIG.

HANNIBAL

HANNIBAL ANTE PORTAS

In the late nineteenth century, the Liebig Company were purveyors of a popular line of beef extract that was used for preparing soups, sauces, stews, and vegetables. As part of their marketing strategy the company—like many others—produced extraordinary sets of trade cards as advertising. The cards were an immensely popular art form, highly imaginative and wide-ranging in subject matter, and exquisitely printed by the sophisticated reproduction technique of chromolithography. They were distributed free to customers with purchase, feverishly collected, and treasured in family albums. The six-part elephant set reproduced on this page and opposite follows an educational tradition: elephants are depicted as amiable workers and fearsome warriors.

L'ÉLÉPHANT: VÉRITABLE EXTRAIT DE VIANDE LIEBIG.

L'éléphant comme bête de trait.

VÉRITABLE EXTRAIT DE VIANDE LIEBIG.

L'ÉLÉPHANT: L'éléphant dans la chasse au tigre.

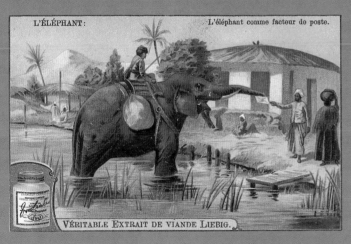

L'ÉLÉPHANT: L'éléphant comme facteur de poste.

VÉRITABLE EXTRAIT DE VIANDE LIEBIG.

weapons in their wars. But certainly the most famous soldiering moment for an elephant corps was under the leadership of Hannibal.

For an attack on Rome in 218 B.C., Hannibal—a general from Carthage—set out from Spain with a huge force of foot soldiers and thirty-seven well-trained elephants. The journey—through the Pyrenees, across the Rhone River, and over the slippery, ice-covered Alps—was hazardous. The elephants were remarkable at thwarting the adversities of nature, particularly in the water, and many of them swam across the Rhone when the rafts capsized. Man and beast made it to the battleground, but the journey had taken its toll. Hannibal's bold military expedition, with its surprising army of bizarre-looking "living tanks," ended in defeat. The Romans captured "The Syrian"—Hannibal's personal mount and the sole elephant survivor—"pardoned" him with an honorable discharge, and retired him to an estate outside Rome, where he became a popular tourist attraction.

Who rides on a tiger can never dismount; asleep on an elephant, that is repose.

—MARIANNE MOORE

THE CAPTIVE'S DREAM

I will remember what I was,
I am sick of rope and chain.
I will remember my old strength
And all of my forest affairs.

I will not sell my back to man
For a bundle of sugar-cane.
I will go out to my own kind,
And the wood-folk in their lairs.

I will go out until the day,
Until the morning break,
Out to the winds' untainted kiss,
The water's clean caress.

I will forget my ankle-ring
And snap my picket-stake.
I will revisit my lost loves,
and playmates, masterless.

—RUDYARD KIPLING

A CAPTIVE PLAYMATE

The affinity between elephants and children must surely be explained by the fact that the animal is so big and so bizarre that to a child it must seem closer to a dream than to reality. The attraction is obviously mutual: playful elephants are ready to scoop up a peanut gently from a tiny outstretched hand and willing to walk about endlessly with packs of small children squealing and squirming upon their backs, retaining their grace and dignity throughout.

A 1940-ish map of the Bronx Zoo in New York City features its most popular attraction on the cover, as does a souvenir package of postal cards from even earlier days, when it was called the "New York Zoological Park."

PERFORMANCE ARTISTS

Some elephants, like some people, are creatures of special and prodigious talent. Exceptional members of the pachyderm family have been widely exploited in nightclubs, theaters, and jungle parks, much to the amusement and amazement of their human audiences.

As part of Frank Bostock's Great Jungle Shows in the early 1900s, Wonder Elephant Mary Ellen was encouraged by her mentor, Herr Scholz, to do laundry on stage. In the 1940s, at the St. Louis Zoo, a pachyderm trio concertized on cello, trumpet, and drum. Ice-skating elephants may be only a figment of

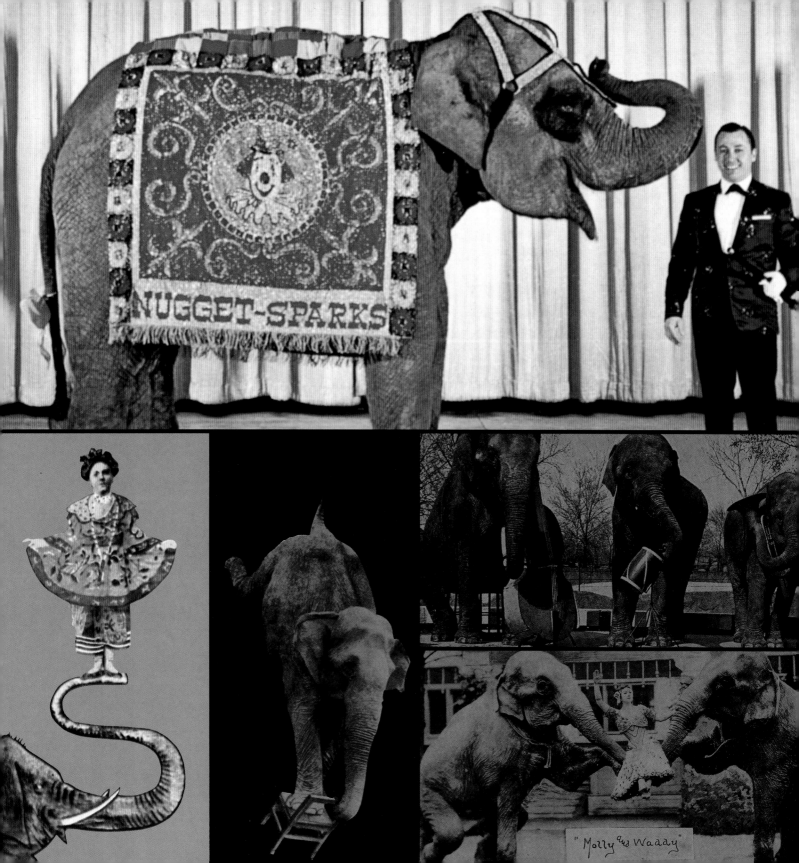

"Molly and Waddy"

Breeding elephants in captivity is difficult. Baby Packy, born in the spring of 1962 at the Portland Zoo, was the first elephant born in the western hemisphere in more than forty years. He was joined in the early '90s by two elephants—Romeo and Juliet—born in Florida into the Ringling circus family of elephants.

A WAY WITH WATER

With the exception of whales, who actually live in water, elephants are the finest swimmers of all mammals. G. P. Sanderson notes in his *Thirteen Years Among the Wild Beasts of India* (1878) that "full-grown elephants swim perhaps better than any other land animals. A batch of seventy-nine…had the Ganges and several of its large tidal brances to cross. In the longest swim they were six hours without touching the bottom; after a rest on a sand-bank, they completed the swim in three more; not one was lost." According to Pliny the Elder's *Natural History*, written during the years A.D. 7–21, an Ethiopian breed was capable of "linking themselves four or five together into a sort of raft and holding up their heads to serve as sails."

artist H. Kley's imagination, but the unusual swing concocted by Molly and Waddy's interlaced trunks is surely not a performing trick to be sneezed at.

Little Bertha, an Asian elephant who was trained from infancy, began performing in 1962 at Nugget's Casino in Reno, Nevada. Thirty years later, no longer little (she now weighs over four tons), Bertha continues her star turn six nights a week, along with her partner, a small elephant called Angel. More than mere performers, these two "goodwill ambassadors" for elephants all over the world are royally cared for. Home is a custom-built "Elephant Palace" featuring its own swimming pool on the Nugget property.

Scientific evidence suggests that elephants themselves, like their closest living relative, the manatee, may once have actually lived in the water. Elephants need water for their physiological well-being and take frequent baths and showers to regulate their body temperature. When the opportunity arises, some have been known to swim almost totally submerged, in a porpoiselike way, using their lifted trunks as snorkels. Be it in a lake, river, stream, or ocean, elephants seem happiest when they are wet.

DAMN EVERYTHING BUT THE CIRCUS!

—E. E. CUMMINGS

THE CIRCUS ELEPHANT

"Clowns and elephants," noted Phineas Taylor Barnum, "are the pegs upon which the circus is hung." But long before Barnum, exhibitions of exotic wild animals were popular. Seafarers returned to the American colonies from their travels across the oceans with lions, camels, tigers, leopards, and polar bears. The first elephant landed on the North American continent in New York Harbor on April 13, 1796. The three-year-old female pachyderm had been purchased for $450 in Bengal, India, by one Captain Jacob Crowninshield. He exhibited the elephant at the corner of Beaver Street and Broadway, where she caused an enormous sensation. A newspaper of the day reported that she "possesses the adroitness of the beaver, the intelligence of the ape, and the fidelity of the dog."

Around 1805, Hackaliah Bailey, a New York State farmer, paid $1,000 for an African female elephant named Old Bet, which his sea captain brother had bought at auction in London for $20. From New York City Harbor Bailey took Old Bet to his home in Somers, stopping along the way to exhibit her for a small fee. Although he had bought Old Bet for farmwork, his journey proved so lucrative that it caused him to change his plan. Bailey bought a wagon and took Old Bet on the road, gradually adding monkeys, a tiger, and a giraffe. The tour became America's first traveling "educational zoological show." Bailey's neighbors quickly became competitors, and Somers became the capital of a "circus fever" epidemic, sending out shows all across the country. The town is renowned as the birthplace of the American circus.

Bailey made a fortune. With the proceeds he built a three-storied brick caravansary in Somers, which he named the Elephant Hotel. After innocent Old Bet was shot to death by a fanatical farmer in 1816, Bailey raised a monument to her in front of his building, a wooden likeness atop a twenty-five-foot-high granite shaft. Today the Old Bet statue still commands the turn in the road, and the hotel across the way from Bailey Park functions as the Somers Town Hall and Historical Society.

By the early 1820s there were more than thirty traveling zoos and menageries touring the United States. Soon, under the brilliant guidance of P. T. Barnum and his competitors, the modern circus was born.

BARNUM, TRAINS, AND THE HEYDAY OF THE CIRCUS

The limitations inherent in the circus's nightly trek through mud and rain in horse-drawn wagons expanded miraculously when the genius of Phineas Taylor Barnum collided with the romance of railroading.

P. T. Barnum spent the first fifty years of his life as the biggest promoter of oddities and curiosities the world had ever known. His American Museum opened on New Year's Day of 1842, and millions came from all over the world to visit. They saw the "Feejee Mermaid"; Joice Heth, George Washington's nurse; Siamese twins Chang and Eng; midget Tom Thumb, scientific rarities; natural exotica; and such attractions as had never before been exhibited.

In 1851 Barnum imported the first herd of elephants to the United States from Ceylon. To announce the opening of his

Great Asiatic Caravan, Museum, and Menagerie, ten of these elephants were harnessed to a chariot and marched along Broadway in New York City. When Barnum sold his interest in the caravan, he kept one elephant as a souvenir, which he settled on a farm near his estate in Connecticut. A portion of the fields, conveniently near the railroad tracks, were plowed by elephant power whenever a train went by. Letters poured in inquiring about the profitability of elephant agriculture. "How much can an elephant draw?" people asked. Barnum's reply: "He can 'draw' the attention of twenty millions of American citizens to Barnum's Museum."

The American Museum was destroyed by fire in 1868, but Barnum rose from the ashes in 1870 to promote the newest wonder of all: a traveling circus on wheels. Joining forces with circusmen W. C. Coup and Dan Costello, he developed what eventually became "The Greatest Show on Earth." To move the gigantic enterprise, Coup dreamed up the circus train. He had specially designed flatcars built, enabling the show to travel comfortably by rail hundreds of miles in a single night, instead of five to fifteen miles along a muddy road.

Circus trains grew increasingly streamlined and efficient. By 1911, with expanded railroad networks, there were close to forty railroad circuses crisscrossing the country. Shows could be bigger and better. One ring exploded into two. Two burst inevitably into three. In the traveling spectacle of the American circus, anything and everything was possible. As the celebrated showman himself declared, "As long as there's babies, there'll be circuses." And a sure way of gauging the health of the circus was, and still is, by the number of elephants.

CIRCUS DAY

Circus Day was once a wildly popular holiday, anticipated as eagerly in Smalltown, U.S.A., as Hallowe'en, Christmas, and the Fourth of July. Weeks before the event, advance advertising "sheets" pasted on trees and barns and telephone poles heralded the mystery and terror and thrills and chills and myriad visions of exotica to come.

Then, one early dawn, a gleaming circus train rumbled in. A vacant dusty lot at the edge of town was transformed into a tented city. Elephants, the strongest and most important helpers, hauled, lifted, pushed, and pulled the poles and canvas into position. Smells of hay, animals, hot dogs, and popcorn wafted through the air. Mud and sawdust were everywhere as the big top emerged above the morning fog.

Rockland, Me. Circus Day.

FRIDAY I TASTED LIFE. IT WAS A VAST MORSEL. A CIRCUS PASSED THE HOUSE.

—EMILY DICKINSON

Back on Main Street, crowds gathered for the grand cortege. At last a drum rolled off in the distance and a band struck up the first notes of "Entry of the Gladiators." The free street parade, an American institution for eighty years, began in an eruption of music, banners, horses, bejeweled equestrian ladies, floats, clowns, and cages of wild animals.

"Hold your horses, here come the elephants!" someone in the crowd cried out as a warning, since the scent of the enormous strange beasts made horses whinny and shy up in terror. The long line of slowly swaying elephants holding "trunk to tail" rumbled by, on their way to the circus tent to perform in "The Greatest Show on Earth." Was it any wonder that this free street parade and the exotic show that followed caused goose bumps and yearning in youngsters all across America, and fear on the part of their parents that their child would be the one to run away from home and join the circus?

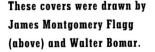

These covers were drawn by James Montgomery Flagg (above) and Walter Bomar.

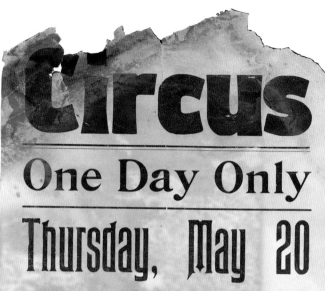

Circus
One Day Only
Thursday, May 20

An Inimitable Ring Master. Plastic, Boneless, Benders and Tumblers. Defying Gyrations on Horizontal Bar. A Dazzling Calisthenic Wand Drill. Prof. Youngsilverpot and Black Beauty. **Two Big Full Brass Bands. The Sensational Mail Bag Mystery.**

Don't Miss The SIDE SHOW MUSEUM

Lillian, the Reptile Charmer	The Wild Man
The Lions, that Teddy Caught	Baby Incubators
The Nigger Dodger	Tattooed Man
Little Jessie, the Mermaid	Smallest Baby in World
The Bearded Lady	Three Armed Lady
Prize Fight	Seven Wonders of the World

Only A Few Seats Left
Now on Sale at Storrs'

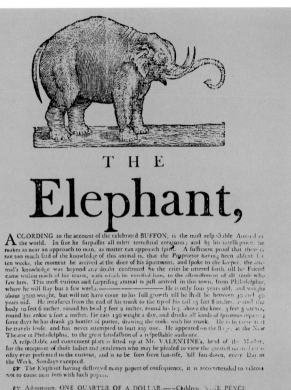

THE
Elephant,

ACCORDING to the account of the celebrated BUFFON, is the moſt reſpectable Animal in the world. In ſize he ſurpaſſes all other terreſtrial creatures; and by his intelligence, he makes as near an approach to man, as matter can approach ſpirit. A ſufficient proof that there is not too much ſaid of the knowledge of this animal is, that the Proprietor having been abſent for ten weeks, the moment he arrived at the door of his apartment, and ſpoke to the keeper, the animal's knowledge was beyond any doubt confirmed, by the cries he uttered forth, till his Friend came within reach of his trunk, with which he careſſed him, to the aſtoniſhment of all thoſe who ſaw him. This moſt curious and ſurpriſing animal is juſt arrived in this town, from Philadelphia, where he will ſtay but a few weeks.———He is only four years old, and weighs about 3000 weight, but will not have come to his full growth till he ſhall be between 30 and 40 years old. He meaſures from the end of his trunk to the tip of his tail 15 feet 8 inches, round the body 10 feet 6 inches, round his head 7 feet 2 inches, round his leg, above the knee, 3 feet 3 inches, round his ankle 2 feet 2 inches. He eats 130 weight a day, and drinks all kinds of ſpirituous liquors; ſome days he has drank 30 bottles of porter, drawing the corks with his trunk. He is ſo tame that he travels looſe, and has never attempted to hurt any one. He appeared on the ſtage, at the New Theatre in Philadelphia, to the great ſatisfaction of a reſpectable audience.

A reſpectable and convenient place is fitted up at Mr. VALENTINE's, head of the Market, for the reception of thoſe ladies and gentlemen who may be pleaſed to view the greateſt natural curioſity ever preſented to the curious, and is to be ſeen from ſun-riſe, 'till ſun-down, every Day in the Week, Sundays excepted.

☞ The Elephant having deſtroyed many papers of conſequence, it is recommended to viſitors not to come near him with ſuch papers.

☞ Admittance, ONE QUARTER OF A DOLLAR.——Children, NINE PENCE.

Boſton, Auguſt 18th, 1797.

BOSTON Printed by D. Bowen, at the COLUMBIAN MUSEUM Preſs,

A broadside illustrated with a primitive woodcut portrait cites the remarkable talents of America's first elephant visitor, on tour throughout the eastern states. The 1797 handbill hawked his feats: "by his intelligence, he makes as near an approach to man, as matter can approach spirit.... some days he has drank 30 bottles of porter, drawing the corks with his trunk."

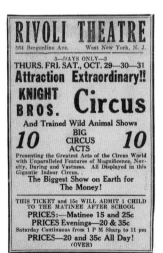

RIVOLI THEATRE
564 Bergenline Ave.   West New York, N. J.

—3 DAYS ONLY—3
THURS. FRI. SAT., OCT. 29—30—31
Attraction Extraordinary!!
KNIGHT BROS. Circus
And Trained Wild Animal Shows
10 BIG CIRCUS ACTS **10**
Presenting the Greatest Acts of the Circus World with Unparalleled Features of Magnificence, Novelty, Daring and Vastness. All Displayed in this Gigantic Indoor Circus.
The Biggest Show on Earth for The Money!

THIS TICKET and 15c WILL ADMIT 1 CHILD TO THE MATINEE AFTER SCHOOL
PRICES:—Matinee 15 and 25c
PRICES Evenings—20 & 35c
Saturday Continuous from 1 P M Sharp to 11 pm
PRICES—20 and 35c All Day!
(OVER)

CIRCUS, N., A PLACE WHERE HORSES, PONIES AND ELEPHANTS ARE PERMITTED TO SEE MEN, WOMEN AND CHILDREN ACTING THE FOOL.

— AMBROSE BIERCE

INSIDE

Old John L. Sullivan, known as "the boxing elephant," was famous for walloping a clown with a boxing glove tied to his trunk. In 1922 the pugilist pachyderm was walked fifty miles from Madison Square Garden to Somers, New York. There, as a tribute, he laid a wreath at the foot of the monument to Old Bet.

In the spring of 1971 the railroad signalmen went on strike. Since the circus train would not cross a picket line, the elephants were forced to walk one and a half miles through the Lincoln Tunnel in a trunk line in order to cross the Hudson River from New Jersey and get to their engagement in New York City at Madison Square Garden. The tollkeeper collected $9.50 for the nineteen elephants— 50 cents each, the going rate for automobiles.

THE BIG TOP

Baby Dumbo trails his mother and aunts in a 1940s postcard.

BALLET OF THE ELEPHANTS

It was 1942, the first wartime circus season and impresario John Ringling North, undoubtedly influenced by Walt Disney's 1940 movie *Fantasia*, dreamed up a "fancy idea" which he proposed to choreographer George Balanchine. The choreographer telephoned Igor Stravinsky. "I wonder if you'd like to do a little ballet with me" asked Balanchine. "A polka, perhaps."

"For whom?" the composer inquired.

"For some elephants," replied Balanchine.

"How old?" asked Stravinsky.

"Very young," Balanchine assured him.

There was a long silence.

"All right," said Stravinsky, "if they are very young elephants, I will do it."

"I did not see this 'ballet for elephants,'" Stravinsky later wrote, "but according to George Balanchine, who choreographed it, the music nearly started a panic, not only among the elephants but also among the musicians of the Ringling Brothers' Circus Band—in an arrangement by someone else: I wrote it for orchestra originally. Vera Zorina, riding at the head of the troupe, must have thought her life was in danger.

"After conducting the orchestra original, in Boston in 1944, I received a congratulatory telegram from Bessie, the young pachyderm to whom the score is dedicated. I did not reply, but when the circus came to Los Angeles, I went to see her and shook her foot."

With pink ballet skirts tied around their ample middles, huge satin bows perched coyly over their ears, the elephants resembled a group of matronly clubwomen "got up" for a little amateur entertainment. It's difficult to be afraid of an elephant when she looks more like the stylish-stout Madame Chairman of an entertainment committee than a savage jungle beast. Ginny (my elephant) even made little bossy sounds at the end of every trick, and I felt sure that if anything went wrong she'd produce a gavel from her ballet skirt and call her "girls" back to order.

—CONNIE CLAUSEN

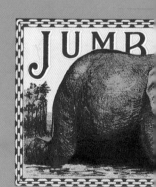

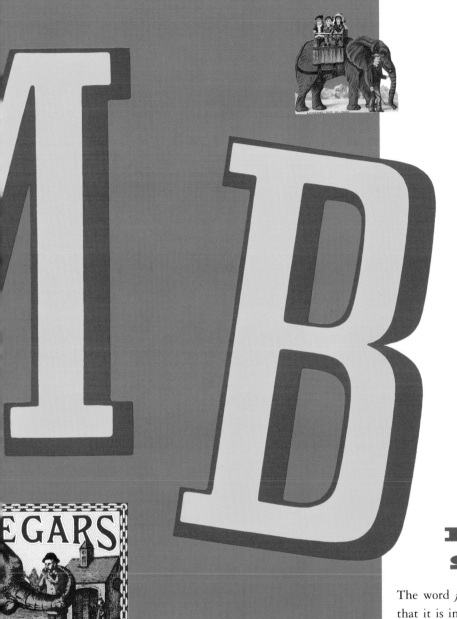

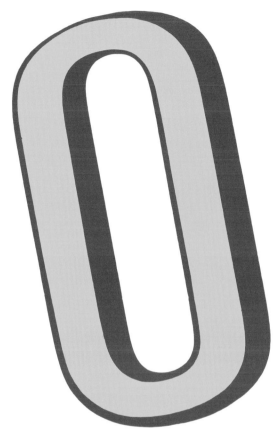

The Elephant Supreme

The word *jumbo* has become so entrenched in popular jargon that it is impossible to imagine the world of advertising without it. It all began with an elephant member of The Greatest Show on Earth, the most popular attraction in circus history.

A bull of the *loxodonta* (African) species, Jumbo was captured as a baby in Ethiopia. After a three-year stay in Paris at Les

Jardins des Plantes, he was traded to the London Zoological Society, in exchange for a rhinoceros and two anteaters. The zoo named him Jumbo, short for Mumbo-Jumbo, and assigned Matthew "Scotty" Scott as his keeper. The two became inseparable.

Jumbo grew in popularity and in size. He was visited by Queen Victoria, Theodore Roosevelt, Winston Churchill, and hundreds of thousands of children and parents who rode in the howdah on his back through the pathways of Regent's Park. After seventeen years, Jumbo had reached the reputed height of twelve feet and weighed six and a half tons. He was the biggest elephant ever held in captivity, and P. T. Barnum wanted him. Barnum offered the zoo $10,000. They accepted.

On Easter Sunday in April of 1882, just in time for the circus opening at Madison Square Garden, Scotty and Jumbo debarked in New York. To throngs of cheering crowds, Jumbo's crate was hauled up Broadway, pulled by a team of horses with two elephants pushing from behind. Although the purchase price and transportation expenses to bring Jumbo to America amounted to $30,000, within six weeks the mammoth—and popular—new circus attraction had more than made up the costs. During his first year, Jumbo earned more than $1 million. Even Barnum was impressed.

> When Jumbo put his foot down on the bridge, as he marched along from New York to Brooklyn, the bridge rebounded after the shock given by his foot. The rebound was met by his second footstep, and there was a great vibration caused by it...it was something terrible to feel that vibration as we walked quietly along the promenade of the bridge. I assure my reader that I was thankful when we arrived on the Brooklyn side.
> —MATTHEW "SCOTTY" SCOTT

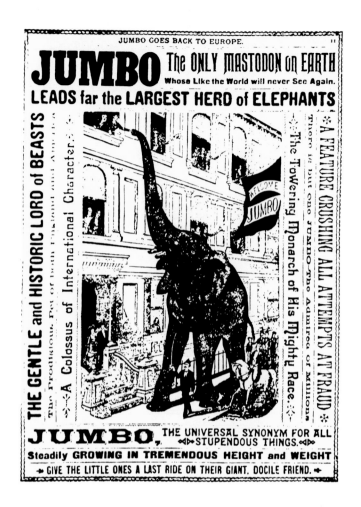

MUTUAL ADMIRATION.

Jumbo's triumphant arrival in New York inspired a barrage of words and pictures. Among them were an 1880 circus poster, above, written in the hyperbolic vernacular of the day, and an amusing drawing by Thomas Nast, in which Barnum happily acknowledges the elephant's superiority in garnering attention.

Jumbomania

JUMBO MUST GO, BECAUSE DRAWN BY WILLIMANTIC THREAD!

This is "JUMBO," but the biggest thing out this season is the "HARTFORD" SEWING MACHINE. WEED S.M. CO. Hartford, Conn., Chicago, Ill. Boston, Mass.

JUMBO REACHING FOR CANDY.

The Best Show Ever Given!

"THE THREE CLOTHIERS,"

THE JUMBO

—OF SPRINGFIELD.—

347 Main Street.

☞ See other side.

Jumbo's departure from London set off a craze of "Jumbomania" on both sides of the Atlantic. The Zoological Garden added $50,000 to its receipts selling Jumbo mementos—medals, canes, neckties, candies, umbrellas, earrings, bracelet charms, fans, perfumes, and pictures—to a population heartbroken with its loss. Restaurants featured Jumbo soups, fritters, bakes, stews, roasts, rolls, patties, pot-pies, hash, puddings, and dumplings. By the time Jumbo arrived in New York, advance publicity had made him a superstar.

Advertisers launched campaigns showing Jumbo at work and play. Trade cards were the most popular advertising media of the day. They were distributed free to customers by retailers or wholesalers and were avidly collected. Barnum encouraged manufacturers to promote their products while also promoting his star attraction.

Companies such as Willimantic Thread, the Hartford Sewing Machine Company, and Smith's Suspender's quickly jumped on the Jumbo bandwagon, using the elephant to stress the strength and power of their products. Clark's O.N.T. Thread commemorated Jumbo's entry to America by producing a set of whimsical cards in which Jumbo appears as a cultured New York City dandy wearing a dapper hat and carrying a personalized suitcase; standing beside a tiny Oscar Wilde, a huge sunflower adorning an imaginary buttonhole; draining an entire barrel of beer at a bar; dressed to the nines at the opera in the exclusive "Horse-Shoe" box; and wearing the latest in swimsuit fashion as he takes to the surf at Coney Island with a baby elephant friend.

Jumbo's influence as a commercial icon set the stage for American advertising's reliance on wild and zoological creatures as logos. Elsie the Cow, Smokey the Bear, the Flying Red Horse, and Tony the Tiger are the direct descendants of the popular pachyderm who towered above them all.

SEE OTHER SIDE

THE WAY JUMBO WAS SUSPENDED.

Messrs. Jos. Wm. Smith & Co.,

Gentlemen.—Your CLINCH BACK SUSPENDERS are appropriately advertised on a "Jumbo" Card, for like the Mastodonic Elephant they are a "big thing." I have used them with great comfort and satisfaction. They are fastened and unfastened as if by magic and your Suspenders are the first that I have worn in twenty years that would not occasionally slip off the shoulders.

Truly yours,

Bridgeport, Conn., May 12, 1882.   P. T. BARNUM

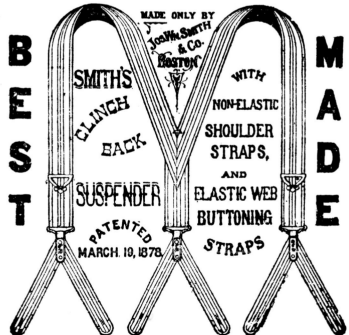

BEST MADE

MADE ONLY BY Jos. Wm. Smith & Co. Boston

SMITH'S CLINCH BACK SUSPENDER

WITH NON-ELASTIC SHOULDER STRAPS, AND ELASTIC WEB BUTTONING STRAPS

PATENTED MARCH. 19, 1878.

Jumbo's Death

On September 15, 1885, The Greatest Show on Earth arrived on its annual railroad tour through the provinces at St. Thomas, Ontario, Canada. As usual, Jumbo traveled in his lavish private "palace" boxcar, which was regally appointed in crimson and gold. After the final performance, as Scotty was leading Jumbo and a dwarf clown elephant called Tom Thumb across the Grand Trunk Railway tracks on the way back to the boxcars, a westbound express struck the two elephants. Tom Thumb sustained no more than a broken leg, but the great Jumbo was hit straight on and died minutes later, holding the hand of his beloved companion Scotty in his trunk.

Ever the master showman, Barnum published his own version of the story: the legend of Jumbo sacrificing his life to save Tom Thumb. Understandably, the public preferred Barnum's tale to the real and gruesome facts. Millions of children and adults mourned Jumbo as a martyr, hero and beloved pet.

Barnum had Jumbo's hide stuffed and mounted—the job took six months—and for two years the dead elephant's effigy led the Barnum and Bailey grand parade. Then the stuffed skin was donated to Tufts University, where Barnum was a trustee and major benefactor. Jumbo's 13-foot-high skeleton was arrayed at the Museum of Natural History in New York City; his heart was donated to Cornell.

Jumbo became Tufts's college symbol and mascot. Tufts's teams are known as the Jumbos; the school yearbook is called *Jumbo*; the image of the elephant is used as an emblem on banners and T-shirts. Tufts even has a song about the immortal pachyderm. Until the stuffed elephant hide was destroyed by fire in 1975, students dropped coins into Jumbo's trunk for good luck. It was reputed to be more effective toward getting an A than all-night cramming.

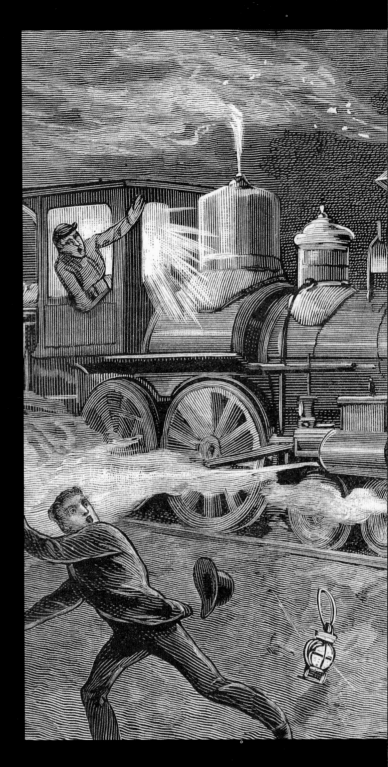

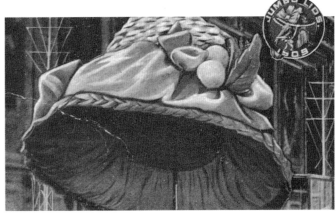

Jumbo·cized

The Jumbo phenomenon did not die in the Ontario train crash. By the early twentieth century, "Jumbo" had become the standard household word for anything oversize. The notion fit in naturally with the American way: more is better, biggest is best.

On the reverse side you see the largest elephant in captivity. We had his picture made on August 17, 1911, at which time the great John Robinson's shows exhibited in our city. We send you this big jumbo card as a reminder that our stock is equally as large and complete as the elephant, and to invite you in to see us. We specialize in Hardware, Furniture, and Stoves. See us before buying. Noland, Jenkins & Wallace
Poplar Bluff, Missouri

"Manhattan's Colossal Novelty," affectionately known as "the Hip," opened at Sixth Avenue between 43rd and 44th streets in 1905. It was the best known and most widely publicized theater on the North American continent when <u>Jumbo</u> exploded on the stage and became a tremendous hit.

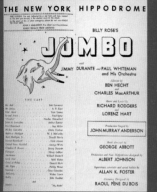

The show gave rise to what became a classic gag, which always brought down the house: When the sherriff arrived on the scene to dispossess the circus and claim the elephant for the rival troupe, Jimmy Durante stood in front of Big Rosie, arms outstretched, and asked, "What elephant?"

"Bigger Than a Show and Better Than a Circus"

In November 1935, Billy Rose, the smallest man on Broadway, opened the biggest show in town at the legendary Hippodrome Theater. He called it *Jumbo*.

Rose, a modern-day Barnum, assembled a legendary team to produce this unique extravaganza, which was part circus, part vaudeville, and part musical comedy. Ben Hecht and Charles MacArthur wrote the play, the story of a rivalry between two circuses. The score by Richard Rodgers, with lyrics by Lorenz Hart, included such classic tunes as "The Most Beautiful Girl in the World," "My Romance," and "Little Girl Blue." As a circus press agent, Jimmy Durante headed a cast of three hundred. Big Rosie, an actress-elephant whose credits included service as a sacred white in Siam, played the title role. There were over a thousand animals—lions, llamas, panthers, horses, zebras, and aardvarks among them—in the cast, all housed in a menagerie in the Hippodrome's newly refurbished basement. Paul Whiteman and his band played for each performance; George Abbott directed.

In 1962, MGM transformed the gigantic stage spectacle into a movie called *Billy Rose's Jumbo*. It starred Mr. Durante from the original cast, along with Doris Day—who learned how to dance while riding bareback on a horse—and a new elephant called Sydney, a trained circus animal from Mississippi. Martha Raye made a special appearance as the woman being shot from a cannon. The film was the Christmas attraction at Radio City Music Hall. Forty years after his death, Jumbo still packed 'em in!

The Woonsocket elephant.

Elephants' positive attributes—strength, power, kindliness, fidelity, memory, wisdom, and longevity—combined with their *jolie laide* looks and appealing, humorous behavior, make them excellent (and inexpensive) spokesanimals. Particularly after the success of Jumbo, elephants began appearing in ads and logos for an astonishing array of products.

The *Graphic* ELEPHANT

IT LOVES IT SO · TRADE MARK

Early American trade cards for soap companies pressed elephants into service as representatives of squeaky clean "ivory" white grooming. A Japanese matchbook company used whimsical elephants at play on their wooden boxes to imply that the matches were sturdy and unbreakable. A French manufacturer of cigarette papers employed a fearsome African male draped in a red cape to suggest the force and resilience of its product.

Elephant logos became widely popular. Five tons of an elephant named Jennie proved so apt at demonstrating a steamer trunk's invincibility that she was incorporated into the company's trademark. A manufacturer of piano ivories used an intensely realistic elephant head as an emblem on the company stationery, while the Woonsocket Rubber company featured the "Elephant Head" on its trademark. Today the tradition continues with the Bazzini's elephant on bags and tins of nuts. And no self-respecting nation is without an elephant postage stamp.

The Smile of the Elephant lurks 'neath a veil

Of mystery yielding no clew,

Like an old-time Professor of Harvard — or Yale —

Who's forgotten to lace up his shoe.

—OLIVER HERFORD

Can we give you a LIFT?

Must be about time for an oil change or lubrication job because it's been 30 DAYS since you've been under our big-top.
Always remember (like the elephant), the cost of oil and grease is peanuts compared to the repair or replacement of parts.

We're as proud of Your Pontiac as you ar

Together we can Protect your Investment, Prolong Your Pride

Fresh Roasted

PEANUTS

Lummis & Co., Inc.

PHILADELPHIA

NET WT. 1.75 OZ.

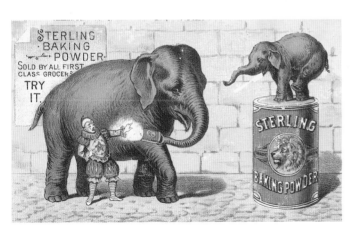

POWER BETHOLINE

JE NE FUME QUE LE NIL

PAPIER A CIGARETTES   JOSEPH BARDOU & FILS

PRODUCE OF U.S.A.

HEFTY BRAND

California VEGETABLES

PACKED AND SHIPPED BY STEWART PACKING CO., SALINAS, CALIFORNIA

HIS TUSKS WERE CLEANED WITH IVORINE

IVORINE IS A BIG THING

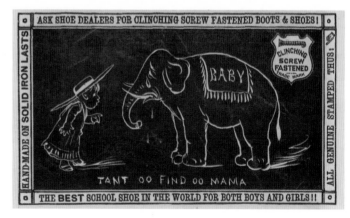

ASK SHOE DEALERS FOR CLINCHING SCREW FASTENED BOOTS & SHOES!

HAND-MADE ON SOLID IRON LASTS

CLINCHING SCREW FASTENED TRADE MARK

BABY

ALL GENUINE STAMPED THUS!

TANT OO FIND OO MAMA

THE BEST SCHOOL SHOE IN THE WORLD FOR BOTH BOYS AND GIRLS!!

THE JUNGLE MATCH
AVERAGE 25   ASPEN STICKS
EXPORT QUALITY MADE IN THE U.S.S.R
REGISTERED TRADE MARK No 950,346

MOGUL   EGYPTIAN CIGARETTES

MADE IN JAPAN

BEST SAFETY MATCHES
KOYEKISHA. MADE IN JAPAN

SAFETY MATCHES
MADE IN JAPAN

TRADE MARK
MADE IN JAPAN

Baseball's Pachyderm

PHILADELPHIA
ATHLETICS

The Philadelphia Athletics Elephant

During the early 1900s, Connie Mack, owner and manager of the original Philadelphia Athletics baseball team, decided to use an elephant as part of the team insignia. This was in response to a disparaging remark by New York Giants manager John McGraw, who regarded the new American League with suspicion and believed teams such as the A's represented nothing more than expensive and problematic "white elephants."

The elephant logo was used on and off for the next half century in Philadelphia and also for a while after the team moved to Kansas City. But when Charlie Finley acquired the team in the early 1960s, he switched to a mule insignia. The current ownership of the Athletics, now known as the Oakland A's, felt the elephant should be restored, symbolizing the club's tradition of looking to the future without forgetting the past.

James V. Lafferty's "Lucy."

THE ARCHITECTURAL ELEPHANT

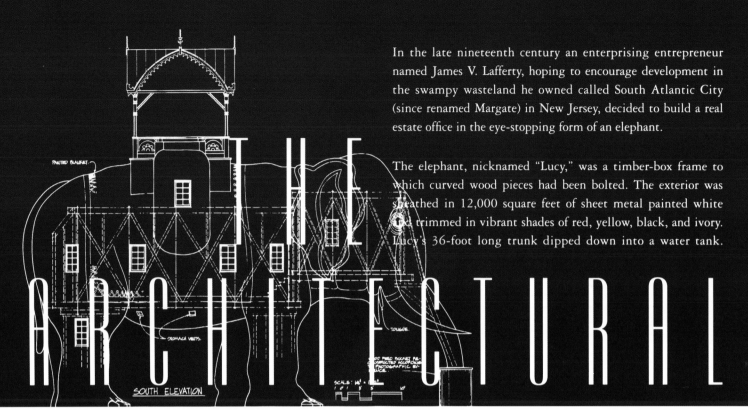

In the late nineteenth century an enterprising entrepreneur named James V. Lafferty, hoping to encourage development in the swampy wasteland he owned called South Atlantic City (since renamed Margate) in New Jersey, decided to build a real estate office in the eye-stopping form of an elephant.

The elephant, nicknamed "Lucy," was a timber-box frame to which curved wood pieces had been bolted. The exterior was sheathed in 12,000 square feet of sheet metal painted white and trimmed in vibrant shades of red, yellow, black, and ivory. Lucy's 36-foot long trunk dipped down into a water tank.

Inside the belly was an office and restaurant; from the six-story-high howdah prospective buyers could gaze out at the panoramic scenery.

The astounding success of Lucy led Mr. Lafferty to build two more elephants. The largest was the Coney Island "Colossus of Architecture," a thirty-seven-room structure billed as "A Whole Summer Resort in a Unique Giant." The building stood 122 feet tall and featured a shopping bazaar and "hotel" rooms in various parts of the elephant's anatomy. The howdah was an observatory complete with two telescopes. People flocked to Coney to book a room for a night of nefarious goings-on in a thigh, hip, shoulder, or trunk. Lafferty's jumbo conceit packed them in from its opening in 1884 until it was destroyed by fire in 1896.

> This remarkable structure is the <u>only</u> one in the world built in this novel shape originated by James V. Lafferty, Philadelphia, who has secured Letter Patent, December 6th, 1882, covering this and all buildings in the shape of Birds, Animals, and Fishes. The building is 87 feet long, 29 feet wide, and 65 feet high, surmounted by a howdah or observatory, from which may be had a magnificent view of the Ocean Bay, Atlantic City, Ocean City, Somers' Point, and adjacent Towns and Villages. The entrance and exit is through the hind legs.

The third and smallest of Lafferty's mimetic buildings was named "Light of Asia," but was popularly known as Jumbo, built in 1885 in Cape May, New Jersey. It was 65 feet high, painted white, and housed a shopping bazaar. Visitors payed ten cents to climb a spiral stair in a hind leg and peek out at the countryside from various windows. Over time, Light of Asia fell into a state of disrepair, and by the turn of the century this marvelous seaside curiosity had been demolished by its owners.

Lucy still looms large over the landscape, however, rescued from destruction and designated a National Historic Landmark in 1976. She remains open to the public, the sole remaining example of a uniquely American "Victorian architectural folly."

Coney Island "Colossus of Architecture."

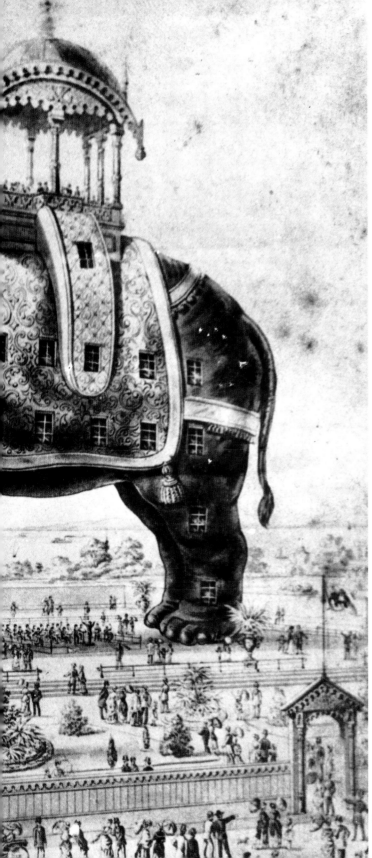

ROYAL ELEPHANTS

In the spirit of the extravagant life-style at the royal court of Versailles, a visionary architect named Charles François Ribart conceived of an appropriately grandiose idea—an elephant palace to be built in the center of Paris in honor of King Louis XV. Designed by Ribart in 1758, "L'Elephant Triomphale" involved a monumental zoomorphic centerpiece surrounded by gardens, fountains, and waterfalls. A statue of the king perched atop the gilded howdah on the elephant's back. The trunk spouted water. Inside was a grand staircase, thermal baths, offices, a theater, the king's throne room in the elephant's head, and a reception hall fashioned to resemble a glen replete with babbling brook.

Ribart's pachyderm palace was never built, but Napoleon revived the plan. At the site of the Bastille in Paris, construction began on the base platform for the gigantic elephant building (today the base supports the Column of July). A model of wood and plaster outlining the structure was begun, and it remained in the square for close to twenty years. The crumbling ruins of the "Grand Kiosque" maquette was home to Le Petit Gavroche, a character in Victor Hugo's *Les Misérables*.

We call it a monument, although it's nothing more than a maquette. But this maquette itself, a magical rough draft, a grandiose cadaver of an idea by Napoleon that two or three successive gusts of wind have carried and tossed each time a little farther away from us, had become historic and had taken on something indefinably definitive that contrasted with its provisional appearance. It was an elephant forty feet high, made of scaffolding covered with masonry, carrying on its back a tower resembling a house, originally painted green by some housepainter, now painted black by the sky, rain, and weather. In this deserted, open corner of the square, the broad front of the colossus, its trunk, its tusks, its tower, its enormous rump, its four legs like columns, created, at night, under a starry sky, a surprising and terrible silhouette. It was hard to know what it meant. It was a sort of symbol of the popular force. It was somber, enigmatic, and immense….a network of cracks fingered their way up its belly, a slat of wood jutted out from its tail, high grasses grew between its legs; and as the level of the square had risen around it over the past thirty years due to that slow, continuous movement that insensibly raises the soil of large cities, it stood in a hollow and it seemed as if the earth had emptied itself out under it. It was huge, despised, repulsive, and superb, ugly to the eyes of the bourgeois, melancholy to the eyes of the thinker. It had something about it resembling a piece of garbage that one might sweep away and something of a king who was about to be beheaded. —**VICTOR HUGO**

GUARDIAN ELEPHANTS

Above, le petit Gavroche, a character in Hugo's Les Misérables, leads two young friends to his "home" in the belly of the Elephant of the Bastille. Right, a dramatic elephant statue residing in the Trocadero Gardens raises its trunk in tribute to a nearby neighbor, Paris's tensile icon, the Eiffel Tower.

Elephant statuary, symbolizing power, peace, and wisdom, is frequently found guarding the entryways to cities, parks, and graveyards throughout the world. In Paris, a realistically carved pachyderm raises his trunk in salute to the Eiffel Tower. A tunnel of rounded elephants lead the way to the Mandarin tombs in China, while two boldly carved elephant columns support the gateway to a boulevard in Copenhagen. Whether constructed of stone, marble, or wood, these massive monuments represent an homage to the gods and a wish for earthly good fortune.

Elephant monuments in Denmark

Bernheimer Japanese Gardens

Mandarin Tombs in China

The <u>Intolerance</u> set

Delhi Gate in India

Elephant Terrace in Cambodia

Fountain in Italy

Albert Memorial in India

Gargoyle in France

PINK & WHITE ELEPHANTS

THE ELEPHANT IS THE

LARGEST ANIMAL YOU'LL

EVER SEE THIS SIDE OF

DELIRIUM TREMENS.

—F. BEVERLY KELLEY

PINK ELEPHANTS

A state of extreme intoxication has been know to cause halluci-nations. These hallucinations can induce thoughts of many strange things, among them, apparently, pink elephants—or so many people in the late nineteenth century believed. That is when the image of pastel elephants—squeezing their heads with their trunks, dancing about the room, hanging from the chandelier, lurking in the closet, curled beneath the rug, and huddled under the bed covers—entered the world of popular culture as a symbol of the condition known scientifically as delirium tremens.

In 1932, Guy Lombardo immortalized the notion of seeing pink elephants while "under the influence" in a popular song written by Mort Dixon and Harry Woods. A few years later, Walt Disney added a creative twist. In his movie *Dumbo*, the

PINK ELEPHANT BAR

PINK ELEPHANT DINING ROOM

baby elephant accidentally gulps down a spiked barrel of water, after which he sees nightmarish visions of camelesque pink elephants singing, cavorting, and marching among the pyramids in the desert.

WHITE ELEPHANTS

After the death of Jumbo, Phineas T. Barnum was anxious to find another elephant attraction for his circus. When he learned that the king of Siam was willing to allow a sacred white elephant out of the country for the right price, a deal was arranged. Three years and $250,000 dollars later, on March 28, 1884, Toung Taloung arrived at New York Harbor.

Journalists on hand for the great event noted that the creature was more dirty gray than snow white and hinted that the elephant might just be a fake. A rival circuser, Adam Forepaugh, claimed to have secured another sacred and truly genuine white elephant. Even when it was discovered that Forepaugh's animal had been painted white, it outdrew the grayish one at Barnum and Bailey's.

So the idiom "white elephant"—signifying a possession entailing great expense out of proportion to its usefulness or value to its owner—entered the American lexicon. It soon grew to symbolize any useless oversize thing or even an unsorted collection of junk. "Anything from a collar button to an elephant," was the way the self-proclaimed Largest Antique and Second-Hand Shop on Earth spelled it out on the side of their White Elephant store in Milford, New Hampshire.

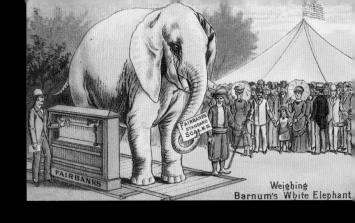

Weighing
Barnum's White Elephant

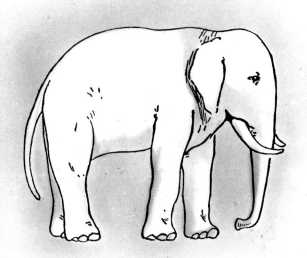

DON'T ALLOW
YOUR FOUNTAIN PEN
TO BECOME

A WHITE ELEPHANT!

REMEMBER I'LL BE
GLAD OF A LINE

A POLITICAL ANIMAL

In the summer of 1874, a New York City newspaper created a sensation when it invented a hoax about wild animals escaped from the Central Park Zoo—all of which created a huge sensation. In November, perhaps inspired by the hoax, political satirist and cartoonist Thomas Nast drew a cartoon inscribed

THE PATRIOTIC ELEPHANT

"An ass, having put on the lion's skin, roamed about the forest and amused himself by frightening all the forest animals he met in his wanderings." Below this, referring to the Democratic nightmare of a third term for General Grant, Nast wrote "Third-Term Panic." The elephant he included, captioned "The Republican Vote," turned out to be the great-great-grandfather of all subsequent GOP elephants.

As a regular contributor to *Harper's Weekly*, Nast created the elephant, donkey, and tiger as symbols of the Republican and Democratic parties and Tammany Hall. Originally, the elephant represented the overwhelming strength of the Republican vote, which dominated the national political arena in the years after the Civil War, but before long it came to stand for the Republican party as a whole.

Since Nast's creation of it in print, the Republican elephant has appeared in innumerable formats.

Thomas Nast's remarkable drawing from <u>Harper's</u>—entitled "Marriage à la Mode"—depicts a formal church wedding in which a carefully coiffed and gowned elephant bride has become permanently entwined with an unknown groom with top hat—undoubtedly a Republican.

Th. Nast.

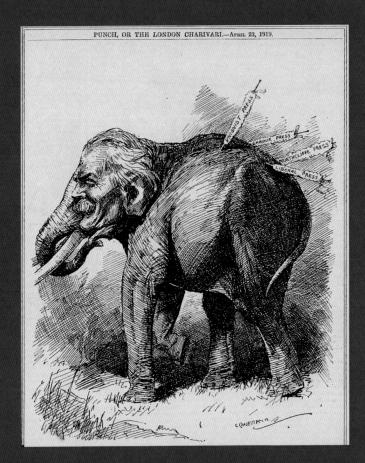

THE
CHEERFUL PACHYDERM

Credit the British humor magazine *Punch* with an original political elephant wrinkle. The eloquent and forceful British statesman David Lloyd George, head of a wartime coalition government, was one of the "Big Four" world leaders at the Paris Peace Talks of 1919. *Punch* portrayed the British prime minister as having skin as resilient and impermeable as an elephant's, to enable him to fend off the criticisms of the unionist, labour, Northcliffe, and liberal presses as he worked for a peace treaty in Paris. As he told Parliament, "I would rather have a good peace than a good press."

From cotton handkerchiefs to metal bumper plates, from bean bags to banners, and on buttons galore, Thomas Nast's joke has been transmogrified into the patriotic symbol of the GOP.

SCHIZOPHRENIC ELEPHANT (BEFORE TREATMENT)

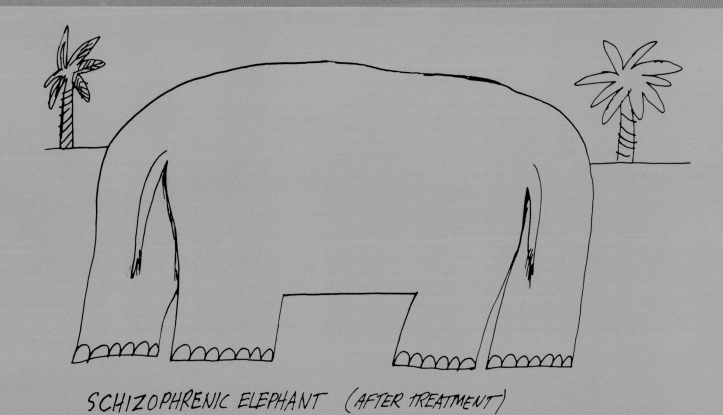

SCHIZOPHRENIC ELEPHANT (AFTER TREATMENT)

Q. What did Tarzan say when he saw the elephants coming?

A. Here come the elephants.

Q. What did Tarzan say when he saw the elephants coming with dark glasses on?

A. Nothing. He didn't recognize them.

It's not that the piano is so old—but the elephant was a very heavy smoker.

—VICTOR BORGE

THE COMIC ELEPHANT

Women are like elephants to me.

I like to look at them,

but I wouldn't want to own one.

—W. C. FIELDS

Q. What weighs 4,000 pounds and sings calypso music?

A. Harry Elefonte.

Q. What happens when you cross an elephant and a jar of peanut butter?

A. Either peanut butter that never forgets or an elephant that sticks to the roof of your mouth.

TWO OLDTIME NEW YORKERS MET ON THE STREET.

"Max," said one, "I have a bargain for you. I can let you have a full-grown elephant for $50."

"Are you crazy?" asked Max. "You know I live in a sixth-floor walk-up with a wife and three kids. What kind of deal is that?"

"Okay, okay," said the first man. "You drive a hard bargain. How about two elephants for $75?"

Max nodded. "Now you're talking."

Q. How can you tell if there's an elephant in bed with you?

A. He has an "E" on his pajamas.

Q. How do you tell an elephant from a banana?

A. Try lifting it. If you can't get it off the floor, it's probably an elephant. But it might be a real heavy banana.

Q. Why do elephants need trunks?

A. Because they don't have glove compartments.

Q. What's gray and comes in a can?

A. Campbell's cream of elephant soup.

Q. Why do elephants lose their teeth in Alabama?

A. That's where the Tuscaloosa.

A Trunk Line.

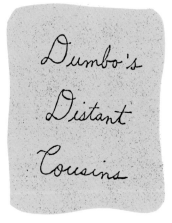

Dumbo's Distant Cousins

BIMBO

Oh, Horace! you are a dear!

" TO THE REFRESHMENT ROOMS, DRIVERSH!"

Q. Why did the elephant cross the road?

A. It was the chicken's day off.

Hey! What's on your mind?

Q. How can you tell if there's an elephant in the bathtub with you?

A. You can smell the peanuts on his breath.

Q. How can you tell if an elephant's been in the refrigerator?

A. Look for his footprints in the cottage cheese.

Q. How do you get six elephants in a Volkswagen?

A. Three in the front seat, three in the back.

RUMBO

MAMBO

DIMBO

RAMBO

R. Chast

You ought to see the other fellow

Let's pack our trunks together

Coax Me

Q. How do you kill a blue elephant?

A. Shoot it with a blue elephant gun.

Q. How do you kill a red elephant?

A. Choke it until it turns blue, then shoot it with a blue elephant gun.

Q. How do you kill a Madras elephant?

A. Shoot it with a water pistol and watch it bleed to death.

Q. Why don't elephants like blue lace petticoats?

A. Who said they don't like blue lace petticoats?

Q. How do you get down from an elephant?

A. You don't get down from an elephant— you get down from a duck.

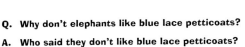

Q. Why are elephants so wrinkled?

A. Did you ever try to iron one?

THE END →

Q. Where do you find elephants?

A. It depends on where you leave them.

RESOURCES

FURTHER READING

AMERICAN HERITAGE EDITORS, NARRATION BY FREEMAN HUBBARD, *Great Days of the Circus*, American Heritage Publishing Co., Junior Library, 1962

PETER BEARD, *Longing for Darkness: Kamante's Tales from Out of Africa*, Harcourt Brace Jovanovich, 1975

EDGAR RICE BURROUGHS, *Tarzan of the Apes*, A. L. Burt Company, 1914

JULIAN CAVALIER, *"Elephants Remembered."* Historic Preservation magazine, Jan–March 1977

CONNIE CLAUSEN, *I Love You. Honey. But the Season's Over*, Holt, Rinehart, Winston, 1961

PAUL B. COURTWRIGHT, *Ganesha Lord of Obstacles. Lord of Beginnings*, Oxford University Press, 1985

JOHN CULHANE, *The American Circus: An Illustrated History*, Henry Holt and Company, 1990

ROBERT DELORT, *The Life and Lore of the Elephant*, Discoveries, Harry N. Abrams, 1992

DR. S. K. ELTRINGHAM, consultant, *The Illustrated Encyclopedia of Elephants*, Crescent Books, New York, 1991

DAN FREEMAN, *Elephants. the Vanishing Giants*, G. P. Putnam's Sons, 1980

CHARLES PHILIP FOX and TOM PARKINSON, *The Circus in America*, Country Beautiful, 1969

David Gucwa and JAMES EHMANN, *To Whom It May Concern: An Investigation of the Art of Elephants*, W. W. Norton & Company, 1985

VERONICA IONS, *Indian Mythology*, The Hamlyn Publishing Group Ltd., 1967

CORITA KENT, *"Damn Everything but the Circus,"* Holt, Rinehart, Winston, 1970

PETER MATTHIESSEN, *African Silences*, Random House, 1991

ANTHONY S. MERCANTANTE, *Zoo of the Gods*, Harper & Row, 1974

E. D. MOORE, *Ivory: Scourge of Africa*, Harper & Bros., 1931

ELAINE MORGAN, *The Aquatic Ape: A Theory of Human Evolution*, Souvenir Press, 1982

CYNTHIA MOSS, *Elephant Memories*, William Morrow & Co., 1988

MARIAN MURRAY, *Circus! From Rome to Ringling*, Appleton-Century-Crofts, 1956

"New York City Ballet Souvenir Book for The Stravinsky Festival," April 6, 1971, reprinted in *A Stravinsky Omnibus*, Alfred A. Knopf, 1972

IVAN T. SANDERSON, *The Dynasty of Abu*, Alfred A. Knopf, 1962

DELIA and MARK OWEN, *The Eye of the Elephant: An Epic in the African Wilderness*, Houghton Mifflin, 1992

JOHN STEWART, *The Circus Is Coming*, The Westminster Press, 1973

HEATHCOTE WILLIAMS, *Sacred Elephant*, Harmony Books, 1989

LAURIE PLATT WINFREY, *The Unforgettable Elephant*, Walker and Company, 1980

ASSOCIATIONS

The P. T. Barnum Museum
820 Main Street
Bridgeport, Connecticut 08804

Circus Fans Association of America
P.O. Box 59710
Potomac, Maryland 20859

Circus Historical Society
3477 Vienna Court
Westerville, Ohio 43081

Circus World Museum
426 Water Street
Baraboo, Wisconsin 53913-2597

Elefriends: The Elephant Protection Group
Cherry Tree Cottage
Coldharbour, Dorking
Surrey, RH5, 6HA, England
Newsletter: *Trunkline*

Elephant Interest Group
106 E. Hickory Grove
Bloomfield Hills, Michigan 48304
Publication: *Elephant*, periodic

Fund for Animals
200 West 57th Street
New York, New York 10019

Hasti Friends of the Elephants
P.O. Box 477
Petaluma, California 94953
Publication: *Hasti Newsletter*, quarterly

International Association of Zoo Educators
c/o Office of Education
National Zoological Park
Smithsonian Institution
Washington, D.C. 20008

Offizielle Postkarte
...gegeben von der Direction des
ZOOLOGISCHEN GARTENS BERL...

International Fund for Animal Welfare
P.O. Box 193
Yarmouth Port, Massachusetts 02675

John Ascuaga's Nugget
P.O. Box 797
Sparks, Nevada 89432
Home of Bertha and Angel, performers
and world ambassadors.

The John and Mable Ringling
Museum of Art
5401 Bay Shore Road
Sarasota, Florida 34243
They have a circus gallery.

Metro Washington Park Zoo
Portland, Oregon 97221
Premier American breeder of Asian
elephants.

National Elephant Collectors Society
38 Medford Street
Somerville, Massachusetts 02145-3810
Publication: *Jumbo Jargon*, quarterly

The Phoenix Zoo
P.O. Box 522191
Phoenix, Arizona 85072-2191
Home of Ruby, Asian elephant who
paints.

Robin des Bois
Association for the Protection of Man
and the Environment
15 rue Ferdinand-Duval
75000 Paris, France

Wildlife Conservation International
A division of the New York Zoological
Society
Bronx, New York 10460

World Blue Chain: for the Protection
of Animals and Nature
39, avenue de Vise
B-1170 Brussels, Belgium

World Society for the Protection of
Animals
Parit Place
10 Lawn Lane, Vauxhall
London SW 8, 1UD, England

The World Wide Fund for Nature
World Conservation Centre
Avenue du Mont-Blanc
CH-1196 Gland, Switzerland

World Wildlife Fund
1250 24th Street
Washington, D.C. 20037

What follows is a listing of some favorites.

The Circus
A 1928 Charlie Chaplin gem with gifted elephant actress Anna May.

Dumbo
Walt Disney's 1941 animated classic.

Elephant Walk
A 1954 film starring Elizabeth Taylor, Peter Finch, and a famous elephant stampede.

Gunga Din
Directed by George Stevens in 1939, starring Cary Grant and Douglas Fairbanks, Jr., in nineteenth-century India.

Ivory Wars
A 1989 documentary produced by the Discovery Channel, available on Home Video.

Billy Rose's Jumbo
A 1962 circus movie with Jimmy Durante (from the original stage production) and Doris Day singing Rodgers and Hart songs.

Tarzan, The Ape Man; Tarzan and His Mate; Tarzan Escapes; Tarzan Finds a Son; Tarzan's Secret Treasure (1932–1941).
Johnny Weissmuller and Maureen O'Sullivan in the original jungle action classics.

ACKNOWLEDGMENTS

Thank you to Roy Finamore, editor supreme, for turning elephant dreams into a concise and cohesive reality; Alexander Isley and Alexander Knowlton for a beautiful creation; Kristen Behrens, who makes everything pleasant and easier; Barbara Hogenson and Beth Gardiner at the Lucy Kroll Agency; Marilyn Furman for her remarkable support and astonishing twenty-year devotion to all things elephantine; Mara Kurtz for her keen design help in getting things started; Andreas Brown at the Gotham Book Mart in New York for his generosity and eagle eye; slidemaster Tom Todd; Ronald W. Meister and Maya Bradford for the amusing elephant jokes; Fred Dahlinger, Jr., at the Circus World Museum; and Annie Gwathmey, Barbara Strauch, Laura and James Johnson, Paula Rubenstein, Faith Coleman, Ricarda O'Conner, John Margolies, Niki and Peter Berg, Suzanne Slesin, Tom West, Ethel Shein, Ellen Stern, and Edward Weinberger for being such a wonderfully supportive family of friends.